CAROLS

for the

Young Choir

CAROLS

for the

Young Choir

Kevin Mayhew

We hope you enjoy the music in this book. Further copies are available
from your local music shop or Christian bookshop.

In case of difficulty, please contact the publisher direct by writing to:

The Sales Department
KEVIN MAYHEW LTD
Buxhall
Stowmarket
Suffolk
IP14 3DJ

Phone 01449 737978
Fax 01449 737834

Please ask for our complete catalogue of outstanding Church Music.

First published in Great Britain in 1997 by Kevin Mayhew Ltd.

ISBN 1 84003 032 1
ISMN M 57004 091 9
Catalogue No: 1450085

1 2 3 4 5 6 7 8 9

Front cover illustration by Piers Harper
Music Editor: Donald Thomson

Printed and bound in Great Britain

Contents

COME TO BETHLEHEM

Text and Music: Alan Viner (b.1951)

Accompaniment preferably for piano

Come to Beth - le-hem and sing your prai-ses to the ba - by who's born for us this

Ah,

night; Je -sus our Sa - viour is sleep - ing sound-ly, while a -

come to Beth -le-hem; Ah, a -

bove, the star shines bright. Ma -ry and Jo - seph look down on the Christ-child,

bove, the star shines bright. Ah,

9

*Optional

rang. Shep-herds a-dore at the man-ger, with cat-tle all a-

rang. Shep-herds a-dore at the man-ger, with cat-tle all a-

round; wor-ship the ti-ny stran-ger, our God with meek-ness crowned.

round; wor-ship the ti-ny stran-ger, our God with meek-ness crowned.

La la la la la la la la la la la la la

Come to Beth - le - hem and sing your prai - ses to the ba - by who's born for us this

la, sing praise to God, la la la la la la la la

night; Je - sus our Sa - viour is the King of Glo - ry and he's

la la la la la la. Ah,

come to bring us light. Joy to the world, and peace to all na - tions,

f *leggiero*

mf *legato, dolce*

sostenuto

bright is the dawn; kneel and a-dore him, wor-ship be-fore him,

bright is the com-ing of the dawn; kneel and a-dore him, wor-ship be-fore him,

Je-sus the Lord is born,

Je-sus the Lord is born,

Je-sus the Lord is born.

Je-sus the Lord is born.

molto cresc.

martellato

8ve ad lib.

THERE WASN'T ANY ROOM AT THE INN

Text: Michael Forster (b.1946)
Music: Christopher Tambling (b.1964)

1. Mary said to Joseph, 'Let's find a place to stay, for it's much too cold to sleep out-side with a ba-by on the way!' There was-n't a-ny room at the inn. There

2. Joseph said to Mary,
   'I hope we'll find a place,
   but the town is full of visitors
   and there's not a lot of space.'

3. Then they found a stable,
   a simple little shed,
   and the Saviour of the world was born
   with a manger for his bed!

For Thomas Hugh Bishop

LULLABY

Text: W.E. Kennedy and S. Uminska
Music: Betty Roe (b.1930)

1. Lul-la-by, Je-sus Child, pearl mine be sleep-ing. Lul-la-by, most be-lov'd,

watch I am keep-ing. Lul-la-by, Je-sus Child.

(or Organ)   Mm,

2. Lul-la-by, Je-sus Child, sleep babe, most sweet-ly, and thou, his mo-ther dear,

mm,

com - fort him meet - ly. Lul-la-by, Je - sus Child.

mm,

mf

3. I'll give thee, Je-sus mine, sweet ber-ries grow - ing, in-to thy mo-ther's heart's

Mm,

mm,

gar - den I'm go - ing. Lul-la-by, Je - sus Child.

mm.

f

4. Bread white and but-ter sweet I'll give thee low - ly, lay - ing them hum-bly in thy

Oo,

oo,

cra - dle ho - ly. Lul-la-by, Je - sus Child.

oo,

Slower

p

5. Hush, hush, the babe doth rest, stilled is his weep - ing.

Mm,

Like a small bird, by his mo - ther he's sleep - ing. Lul-la-by, Je - sus

mm,

mm,

rall.

Child.

pp

mm,

pp

THE STABLE WHERE THE OXEN STOOD

The Manger Bright

Text: Madeline Chase (b.1902)
Music: William Lloyd Webber (1914-1982)

lan - tern shone the ho - ly light on Ma - ry, and the man - ger bright which

held her ba - by son, which held her ba - by son.

Here Je - sus lay, a lit - tle child, the

three kings came to see, to wor - ship with their gifts most rare our

Sa - viour Lord to be. Dear Jesus, bless us from a-bove, and all our pets, and those we love, bless our Christ - mas song to thee, our Christ - mas song to thee, our Christ - mas song to thee.

RAGTIME CAROL

Text: adapted from George Ratcliffe Woodward (1848-1934)
Music: Christopher Tambling (b.1964)

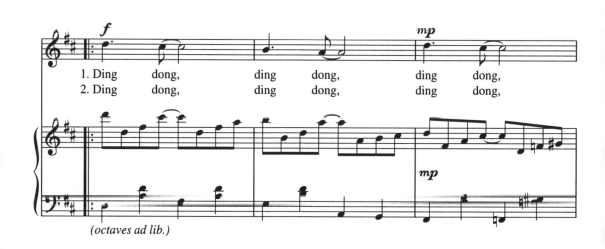

1. Ding dong, ding dong, ding dong,
2. Ding dong, ding dong, ding dong,

(octaves ad lib.)

ding dong. Up! good Chri - stian folk, and list - en
ding dong. Tell the sto - ry how from glo - ry

how the mer - ry church bells ring,
God came down at Christ - mas time,

and from stee - ple
bring - ing glad - ness,

bid good peo - ple come and a - dore the new - born king.
chas - ing sad - ness, show - er - ing bless - ings far and wide.

3. Ding dong, ding dong, ding dong,

A DAY OF GLORY

Text: John Mason Neale (1818-1866)
Music: Andrew Moore (b.1954)

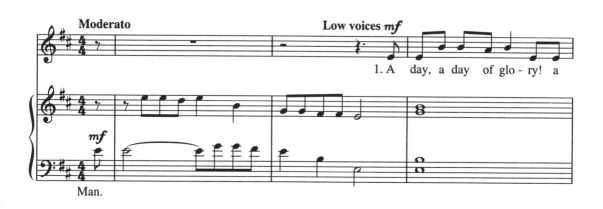

day that ends our woe! a day that tells of tri - umph a - gainst our van - quished foe! Yield

sum - mer's bright - est sun - rise, to this De - cem - ber morn: lift up your gates, ye prin - ces, and

Verses 2 and 4 may be sung with equal or unequal voices.

prince of wine and corn: lift up your gates, ye prin - ces, and

birth - place, the prince of wine and corn: lift up your gates ye

let the child be born.

prin - ces and let the child be born.

mf *dim.*

Very much slower
High voices *p*

3. Then bar the gates, that hence-forth none thus may pas-sage win, be -

Solo

Sw. *p*

cause the Prince of Is – rael a – lone hath en – tered in. The

earth, the sky, the o – cean his glo – rious way a – dorn: lift

up your gates, ye prin – ces and let the child be born.

GOD WAS BORN ON EARTH

Never mind the sheep, look for the baby

Text: Michael Forster (b.1946)
Music: Andrew Gant (b.1963)

1. God was born on earth a home-less stran-ger, fac-ing ev-'ry kind of mor-tal dan-ger scrounged him-self a bed in a don-key's man-ger in the town of Beth-le-

2. Shepherds in the fields with sheep to care for,
   angels said, 'What are you sitting there for?
   Never mind the questions, the whys and wherefores,
   get along to Bethlehem!'

3. Never mind the sheep, look for the baby,
   he's the one to watch, I don't mean maybe.
   If you want to share in the special day, be
   sure to go to Bethelehem.'

4. So they left the sheep and went out looking,
   eager to find out what God had cooking,
   found a classic problem of overbooking
   in the town of Bethelehem.

5. Jesus doesn't put on airs and graces,
   likes to be in unexpected places,
   comes to us in smiles and warm embraces,
   as he did at Bethelehem.

For the Johnstown Junior Choir

UNTO US IS BORN A SON

Text: George Ratcliffe Woodward (1848–1934)
Music: Colin Mawby (b.1936)

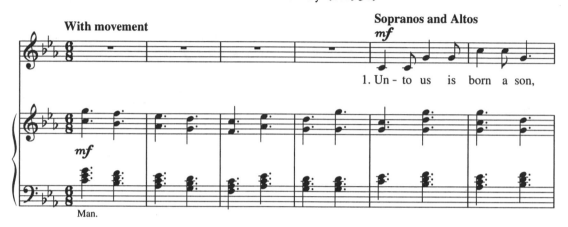

Altos (or Men)

2. Christ, from heav'n de - scend - ing low, comes on earth a stran - ger:

ox and ass their own - er know be - cra - dled in a man - ger, be - cra - dled

in a man - ger.

All ff

3. This did He - rod

sore af - fray, and grie - vous-ly be - wil - der; so he gave the

word to slay, and slew the lit - tle chil - der, and slew the lit - tle

Altos (or Men) *mf*

chil - der.   4. Of his love and mer - cy mild

Man.

this the Christ-mas sto - ry: and O that Ma-ry's gen - tle child might lead us up to

glo - ry, might lead us   up to glo - ry!

HEE, HAW! HEE, HAW!
The donkey's Christmas carol

Text: Michael Forster (b.1946)
Music: Noel Rawsthorne (b.1929)

young to re - al - ise he's get - ting in the way!

I don't blame the ba - by, not his fault at all, but his

par - ents should re - spect a don - key's feed - ing stall!

D.C.

2. After all that journey,
   with my heavy load,
   did I ever once complain about the dreadful road?
   I can cope with backache,
   and these swollen feet.
   All I ask is some respect, and one square meal to eat.

3. 'Be prepared,' I told them,
   'better book ahead.'
   Joseph said, 'Don't be an ass,' and took a chance instead.
   Now they've pinced my bedroom,
   people are so rude!
   I can cope with that, but not a baby in my food!

LULLABY OF THE NATIVITY

Text: from the 'Sloane' Manuscript
Music: James Patten (b.1936)

For the Glenalmond Choral Society

CHARLESTON CAROL

Text: Traditional English
Music: Christopher Tambling (b.1964)

Accompaniment preferably for piano

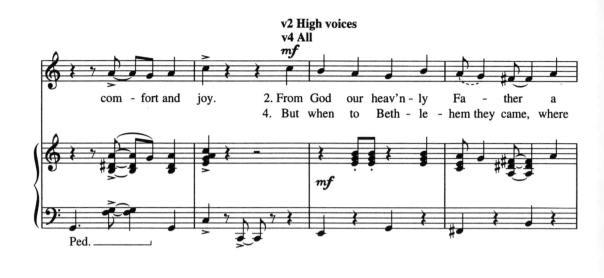

v2 High voices
v4 All

com - fort and joy.   2. From God   our heav'n - ly   Fa - ther   a
4. But when   to   Beth - le - hem they came, where

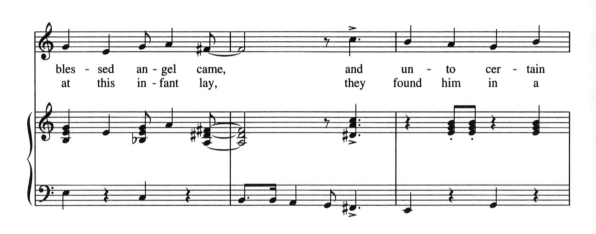

bles - sed   an - gel   came,   and   un - to   cer - tain
at   this   in - fant   lay,   they   found   him   in   a

(optional SATB)

shep - herds   brought   ti - dings   of   the   same,   How
man - ger,   where   ox - en   feed   on   hay;   His

that in Beth - le - hem was born the Son of God by name: O
mo - ther Ma - ry kneel - ing, un - to the Lord did pray: O

cresc.

f

ti - dings of com - fort, com - fort and joy, O

f

f

1.

Low voices

ti - dings of com - fort, com - fort and joy! 3. The

Ped. _____

45

For the Johnstown Junior Choir

IN THE BLEAK MID-WINTER

Text: Christina Rossetti (1830-1894)
Music: Colin Mawby (b.1936)

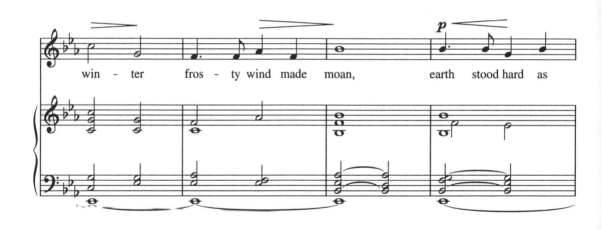

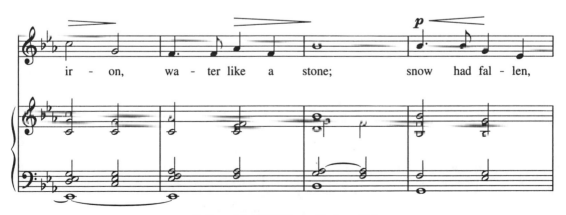

snow on snow, snow on snow, in the bleak mid -

win - ter, long a - go, long a - go.

Our God, heav'n can - not hold him

nor earth sus - tain; heav'n and earth shall flee a - way

Man.

Ped.

when he comes to reign. In the bleak mid - win - ter a

sta - ble - place suf - ficed the Lord God Al - migh - ty,

Je - sus Christ, Je - sus Christ.

Optional descant *pp*

All

Oo,

What can I give him, poor as I am?

If I were a shep - herd I would bring a lamb;

if I were a wise man I would do my part, yet what I can I

give him: give my heart, give my heart, my heart.

EVERYONE'S A CHRISTMAS BABY

Text: Sarah Forth
Music: Noel Rawsthorne (b.1929)

God is smil-ing up at us from ev-'ry girl and boy. Yes!

D.S.

2. Christmas comes on ev'ry day,
   and in ev'ry kind of place,
   for each new child that's born on earth
   reveals God's love and grace. Yes!

3. Life and hope begin anew
   when another child is born,
   and ev'ry morning that we awake
   is like a new world's dawn. Yes!

For the Poole Schools Music Association

THE HOLLY AND THE IVY

Text: Traditional English
Music: Malcolm Archer (b.1952)

For Treble voices

deer, the play-ing of the mer-ry or-gan, sweet sing-ing in the choir.

2. The hol-ly bears a blos-som as

white as the li-ly flower, and Ma-ry bore sweet Je-sus Christ to be our sweet sa-

viour. Oh, the ri-sing of the sun, and the run-ning of the deer, the

good. Oh, the ri-sing of the sun, and the run-ning of the

good. Oh, the ri-sing of the sun, and the run-ning of the

deer, the play-ing of the mer-ry or-gan, sweet sing-ing in the choir.

deer, the play-ing of the mer-ry or-gan, sweet sing-ing in the choir.

4. The hol-ly bears a

pric-kle as sharp as a-ny thorn and Ma-ry bore sweet Je-sus Christ on Christ-mas Day in the morn. Oh, the ri-sing of the sun, and the run-ning of the deer, the play-ing of the mer-ry or-gan, sweet sing-ing in the choir.

all. Oh, the ri-sing of the sun, and the run-ning of the

all. Oh, the ri-sing of the sun, and the run-ning of the

sub. **p** *cresc.*

deer, the play-ing of the mer-ry or-gan, sweet sing-ing in the choir.

sub. **p** *cresc.*

deer, the play-ing of the mer-ry or-gan, sweet sing-ing in the choir.

sub. **p** *cresc.*

6. The hol-ly and the

i - vy when they are both full grown of all the trees that are in the wood the

hol - ly bears the crown. Oh, the ri- sing of the sun, and the run-ning of the

deer, the play-ing of the mer-ry or -gan, sweet sing - ing in

the choir!

the choir!

WHEN CHRIST WAS BORN OF MARY FREE

Text: 15th Century
Music: Rosalie Bonighton (b.1946)

2. Herd-men be-held these an - gels bright to them ap-pear-ed with great light, and said, 'God's son is born this night': in ex-cel-sis glo-ri-a, glo-ri-a, glo-ri-a, in ex-cel-sis glo-ri-a.

3. This
Man.

king is come to save his kind, in the scrip-ture as we find; there-fore this song we

Ped.

have in mind: in ex-cel-sis glo-ri-a, glo-ri-a, glo-ri-a, in ex-cel-sis

glo-ri-a. 4. Then, dear Lord, for

thy great grace, grant us the bliss to see thy face, where we may sing to thy so-lace: in ex-cel-sis glo-ri-a, glo-ri-a, glo-ri-a, in ex-cel-sis glo-ri-a.

rall.

MARY HAD A BABY

Text and Music: Traditional West Indian
Arranged by Christopher Tambling (b.1964)

train has gone! 2. What did she name him, yes, Lord,
4. Where was he born, yes, Lord,

what did she name him, yes, my Lord,
where was he born, yes, my Lord,

what did she name him, yes, Lord!
where was he born, yes, Lord! The

peo-ple keep a-com-ing, but the train has gone! train has gone!

where did she lay him, yes, Lord! The peo-ple keep a-com-ing, but the

train has gone! 7. Laid him in a man - ger,

yes, Lord, laid him in a man - ger,

yes, my Lord, laid him in a man - ger,

yes,   Lord!   The peo - ple keep   a - com - ing, but   the

train   has   gone!